Amen, Brother Ben

AMEN, BROTHER BEN

A Mississippi Collection of Children's Rhymes

By Marice C. Brown

 University Press of Mississippi
JACKSON

Copyright © 1979 by the University Press of Mississippi
Manufactured in the United States of America
All Rights Reserved
Designed by James J. Johnson
Illustrations by Ken Nichols

This volume is sponsored by the
University of Southern Mississippi
Hattiesburg, Mississippi

Library of Congress Cataloging in Publication Data
Main entry under title:

Amen, brother Ben: a Mississippi collection of children's
    rhymes.
    1. Folk-lore and children—Mississippi.   2. Games—
Mississippi.   3. Counting-out rhymes—Mississippi.
4. Jump rope rhymes—Mississippi.
I. Brown, Marice C.   II. Title.
GR110.M7A47   398.8   78–32017
ISBN 0–87805–094–9

for all children everywhere, but especially for
Kay and Leigh,
who were children only yesterday

Acknowledgments

The volume presented here is the result of assistance from scores of people. Collections of this kind present particular difficulties in acknowledging sources, that is, the informants themselves. I express my gratitude to numerous persons whom I have never seen, as well as to those whom I have, for being willing participants in recalling childhood games.

Some individuals who were most helpful must be acknowledged. The late Jack A. Smith was particularly encouraging. Many of my graduate students collected information from their own students throughout the state. I am indebted to Shirley Guy, Carolyn Murphy, Augustine McPhail, Ruth Campbell, Margaret Bice, Mary Peddicord, Gwendolyn Porter, and Elaine Hughes. In addition I remember many classmates and friends of my own early school years who made the learning of a host of rhymes, games, and riddles part of my childhood. Finally, I remember with tenderness the games my parents taught me.

Contents

Preface

Many years ago when my son was a small boy, he called me to his bedside to ask if he could pray to the devil when he had finished his prayer to God. Surprised, certainly, but also amused, I consented, mainly to find out what was going on in that youthful brain. He said his short ritualistic prayer, and then came his prayer to the devil:

Amen, Brother Ben,
Shot a goose
And killed a hen.

Whether the wild irrelevance or the significance of the recital was the more compelling reaction is hard to determine now. In either case the incident directed my attention to the fascinating topic of folklore and more specifically to child lore. How children transmit lore from one to another and how the same rhymes and games appear generation after generation, though often in variant forms, remain endlessly attractive. Moreover the answers to these questions have deeper importance to the development of the child than appears initially.

Partly as a result of the interest sparked by the incident related above, I began collecting children's rhymes and jingles about a decade ago, working somewhat spasmodically and without any specific goal. As the collection grew, so did my interest, and I determined to delimit the geographical area and the *informants,* or persons recalling the item. The collection was to be representative only of Mississippi. Furthermore, the person from whom I got the item must have lived in the state between the years of four to fourteen. In setting that limit, I was following the practice of William Labov, a linguist who had done an extensive study on peer pressure in language acquisition (specifically, dialect).

Labov found that a child's peers were more influential on the kind of dialect the child used than either the school or the home. Age four is about the lowest age at which a child comes into contact with his peers. By age fourteen he has passed the period of greatest peer pressure on his speech. It seemed to me then that since those same years coincided with the most intense period of group play, both supervised and unsupervised, the collection of folk items would be valuable not only for the artifacts themselves but also for any variants that might occur.

During the period of collecting, I accepted items from any source whatever, but I insisted on knowing where the informant lived during the years of four to fourteen and the approximate year when he learned the item.

All items went into a card file. When I began the actual compiling of the items enclosed in this book, I laid aside all entries that did not fulfill the two requirements stated above. At another time they may prove valuable in a comparative study of child lore.

When time to organize the collection came, further reduction was needed. Recitals of doggerel occur as a minor part of a great many games, but they are not integral to the game. Or, if the language is a necessary part of the game, as in "May I?" it is not verse or recited in a strong cadence. The latter situation is true of riddles, where the conundrum is couched in colloquial language rather than in verse. The remaining part of the collection was divided into four categories: count-outs, jump-rope rhymes, autographs, and jeers and taunts. In cases where there are optional lines, they have been appended in parentheses to the verses. Also, in those cases where verses were clearly variations of a common form, I arbitrarily selected one as a base form and incorporated the variants in the footnotes.

If the reader's imagination is sparked by the following rhymes and jingles, the memory quickened and the day somehow brightened—then this book will have achieved its purpose.

Amen, Brother Ben

1
COUNT-OUT RHYMES

THE SINGLE MOST IMPORTANT, as well as the most fascinating, aspect of child play may well be the psychological and sociological factors involved in the use of an "It" as a central figure in many children's games.

The Reverend Walter Gregor points out that count-outs are a type of lottery in which an individual may account to chance, or fate, what he might otherwise have to bear responsibility for.[1] History and literature are rife with examples. An instance in modern times is the execution of a traitor by a squad whose guns, except one, are filled with blanks in an effort to remove guilt from any single individual and to ascribe to chance the actual executor.

One clear bit of evidence supporting the claim that free play among children, as opposed to supervised school-ground or park recreation, is fast disappearing lies in the dearth of modern count-outs. Gregor, for example, published hundreds of count-outs in use in the latter part of the nineteenth century, nearly all nonsense or riddled with lines of nonsense. Typical of the form is the rhyme below.

> Onery, twoery, tickery, tock,
> Alliby crackiby, ten or eleven,
> Peem, pam, musky, dan,
> Tweedlum, twadlum, twenty-one.

1. Walter Gregor, *Counting-Out Rhymes of Children* (Darby, Pa.: Norwood Editions, 1973), 6–9. The collection cited is printed from a paper read to the Buchan Field Club in Peterhead, England, 1889. The folklorist gives an extremely interesting history of the lottery as a form of prognostication as well as a stroke of chance.

It seems obvious that some of the language is pure verbal and rhythmic play. "Onery, twoery, tickery, tock" has a satisfying meter and suffix repetition. The second and third lines, however, leave one curious about possible analogs in other oral literature that predates the count-outs. Little has been done to search out possible correlates, though Gregor makes some tentative suggestions of great interest.

Count-out rhymes verbalize the act of making a selection of participants in a game: "Out goes you,[2] you old dirty dishrag, you." The children gather in a circle or stand in a row and a leader supervises the count-out. If the game is one in which sides are drawn, a count-out may be eliminated in favor of two leaders, usually self-appointed, who choose the members of each group, naming them alternately until all players are selected. If, however, the game is one in which a single person is pitted against the group, an It must be selected. The cry of "Let's play 'May I?'; I'm It!" secures the honor; but if, as often happens, the role of It is one of victimization, then cries of "Not It!" rend the air and the last child to be heard must accept the assignment.

A far more common method of selection is the reciting of a count-out verse. A child, likely the same one who suggested the game, takes the leader's position. Starting with himself, he recites a rhyme in strong cadence pointing on the stressed syllables to each child in turn. The person he is

---

2. "Out *goes you*" is an interesting form, likely a dialectal Scottish form.

pointing to on the last stress is It. In some cases, however, the count-out eliminates one child at a time and the one left in the circle or row becomes It. The drawing out of the selection process certainly indicates that the actual selection is a pleasant part of the game. Many contributors of count-outs confirmed the fact that it was advantageous to know many verses so that a counter could go from one to another until the final stress fell on a favored, or if the role were unpleasant, a disfavored player.

It appears also, in the United States at least, that count-outs came to be used rather specifically for certain games. "One Potato" is largely restricted to boys and ball games, since there is an accompanying ritual of grasping the bat, one player's hand over the other, until the bat has been "measured." On the other hand, "Eenie, meenie, minie, moe" is preferred as a selection for round games—"Drop the Handkerchief," for example.

The collection presented here lacks the quaintness of older collections. It has a practical tone and a flippancy suitable for modern children. But the mere fact that count-outs still exist underscores the psychological complexity inherent in the selection of an It, whether the role victimizes or honors the child whom "Fate" selects.

1. _____ horses in a stable
    Start at the highest number of children playing.
  Six horses in the stable and one jumped out.
  Five horses in the stable and one jumped out.
  Four horses in the stable and one jumped out.
    The child designated number one is It.

2. A bushel of wheat, a bushel of rye,
  All ain't hid, holler I.

3. A mouse built a house.
  How many bricks did he use?
    On the word "use" the counter will touch a player who will designate a number, say "nine." The counter will count up to the ninth person, who will then be out.

4. A sailor went to sea, sea, sea
  Just to see what he could see, see, see;
  But all that he could see, see, see
  Was the bottom of the sea, sea, sea.

5. Akka bakka, soda cracker,
  Akka bakka boo,
  Akka bakka, soda cracker,
  Out goes you.

6. Apples, peaches, pears, and plums;
   Tell me when your birthday comes.
   Answer: J-A-N-U-A-R-Y.

   > *The person pointed to on "comes" spells out the month in which his birthday falls and the count-out continues.*

7. Blue shoe, blue shoe,
   How old are you?
   Answer: Eight (or appropriate number).

   > *The counter counts up to eight and the person on whom the number falls is out.*

8. Bubble gum, bubble gum, in a dish,
   How many pieces do you wish?

   > *Player answers any number. Example: Ten.*

   1, 2, 3, 4, 5, 6, 7, 8, 9, 10, and you are not It.

   > *Player steps out, and the same procedure continues until only one is left.*

   . . . and you are It.

9. Eenie, meenie, minie, moe,
   Catch a monkey[3] by the toe;
   If he hollers, make him pay
   Fifty dollars[4] every day.

   ---

   3. Variants: nigger; rabbit; tiger; Old Tojo; Hitler
   4. Variants: fifteen; twenty; a hundred

10. Engine, engine, number nine,
Going down the railroad line,
If the train runs off the track,
Do you want your money back?

>   *The person pointed to on the word "back"
>   answers "yes."*

Y-E-S spells *yes*, and you are (not) It.

>   *Sometimes the children stand in a marked
>   circle, and step outside as they are counted
>   out.*

11. I struck a match and it went out.

>   *The person on whom the last word ends is
>   out, and the chant is repeated until only one
>   is left in. He is It.*

12. Ikki bikki, soda cracker,
Does your mama chew tobacco?
Ikki bikki, soda cracker,
Out goes you.

13. Ink, stink, bottle of glue,
All out but you.

14. Intery, mintery, cutery-corn,
    Apple seed and apple thorn;
    Wire, briar, limber-lock,
    Five geese in a flock.
    Sit and sing by a spring,
    O-U-T, and in again.

15. Little boy, driving cattle,
    Don't you hear his money rattle?
    One, two, three,
    Out goes she!

16. Money, monkey, bottle of beer,
    How many monkeys have we here?
    One, two, three.
    Out goes he!

17. My mother and your mother were hanging out the
        clothes.
    My mother gave your mother a punch in the nose.
    What color was the blood?
    Blue—
    B-L-U-E spells *blue*, [5] and out you go.
    With a jolly good clout on your nose.

    _____

    5. Variants: Y-E-L-L-O-W spells yellow; R-E-D spells red

18. My mother told me to pick this (very best) one (and you are It).

19. One for the money
     Two for the show,
     Three to make ready
     And four to go.

20. One potato, two potatoes, three potatoes, four;
     Five potatoes, six potatoes, seven 'taters more.
     Repeat until you come to the last person in the group. Then cry, "You're out!"

21. One, two, buckle my shoe,
     Three, four, shut the door.
     Five, six, pick up sticks.
     Seven, eight, close the gate.
     Nine, ten, you're a big fat hen.[6]

22. One, two, three,
     Mother caught a flea,
     Flea died and mother cried.
     One, two, three.

---

6. Variant: Nine, ten, start again.

23. One, two, three, four, five,
    Once I caught a fish alive,
    Six, seven, eight, nine, ten,
    Then I let it go again
    Why did you let it go?
    Because it bit my finger so.
    Which finger did it bite?
    The little finger on the right.

24. Out goes the cat,
    Out goes the rat,
    Out goes the lady with the blue straw hat.

25. O-U-T goes you old dirty (dish)rag.
    My mother told me to pick this one.

26. Three little monkeys in a coconut shell,
    One could read, one could write,
    One could smoke his daddy's pipe.
    O-U-T spells *out* you dirty dishrag you.

27. Tich, tach, touch blue
    This goes out along with you.

28. Two pounds of washing powder,
    Two pounds of soap.
    All ain't hid is a billy goat.

29.   William A. Trembletoes[7]
       He's a good fisherman,
       Catches fish(es)
       Puts 'em in (a) dish(es)
       Catches hens,
       Puts 'em in pens,
       Some lay eggs,
       Some lay none,
       Wire, briar, limberlock
       Three geese in a flock;
       One flew East
       And one flew West,
       And one flew over the cuckoo's nest.
       O-U-T spells *out*;
       Go out you dirty dishrag, you.

---

7. Variant: William, William, Trembletoes.

2
JUMP-ROPE RHYMES

"Hot pepper!"

As A GAME, jump-rope has a distinct advantage in that it permits team play of a low organizational type, but it may also be played by a single jumper who holds both ends of a rope and swings it in an overhead arc, jumping over the rope as it completes the circle under his feet. With a slightly longer rope, one end may be tied to a post, tree, or upright support and the other end swung by a player. Two players are a minimum number for this kind of game: one "turns" while the other jumps. With three or more players, they must take turns, two turning the rope while the other(s) jumps. Depending on the length of the rope, two or more children may jump together. Furthermore, this versatile game may permit the player to stand in the appropriate spot and start jumping when the rope completes its first arc or run in and out while the rope is in full swing. Needless to say, the latter situation requires more skill, both on the part of the jumper and the rope "turners." In addition, the jumpers perform various embellishments in accord with the words chanted, in a manner somewhat reminiscent of the familiar square dance "calls." The "Teddy Bear" verse (verse 57) is a good example. Finally, the rope may be turned at various speeds and everywhere English is spoken the cry of "Hot pepper!" is a call for extremely fast jumping. Coordination among all active players—both jumpers and turners—is necessary, and verses chanted by all participants provide the necessary rhythm.

Jump-rope verses themselves reflect the physical and social changes taking place in the development of the child. Since skill is to be measured, a count must be kept of the number of jumps the player has before he "misses," or stumbles on the rope. In these cases it is instructive to note the kinds of information that precede the count. How many kisses she received; whether she will eventually be the mother of single children, twins, or triplets; the initials of her lover; the occupation of her future husband—all these matters clearly indicate that although boys may not often be direct participants in the game, they are very much in the minds of the girls. In former days such frivolity would not have been tolerated as a topic of conversation—at least in the presence of adults—but the guise of a game made it permissible. Modern children have no such restrictions placed on them, but the pleasure in the rhythmic chants seems to linger.

1. _____, _____, turn around,
    _____, _____, touch the
    ground,
    _____, _____, say your A-B-Cs,
    A, B, C, . . .
    Until the jumper misses.

2. Amos and Andy, sugar and candy,
    Ice, spice, IN.
    The player runs in.
    Amos and Andy, sugar and candy,
    Ice, spice, DOWN.
    The player stoops to touch the ground.
    Amos and Andy, sugar and candy
    Ice, spice, UP.
    The player raises his arms high.
    Amos and Andy, sugar and candy,
    Ice, spice, OUT.
    *The player runs out of the circle of the turn-
    ing rope.*

3. Apples, peaches, pumpkin pie,
    How many years before I die?
    One, two, three . . .
    The count continues until the jumper misses.

4. Aunt Dinah's dead.
    How'd she die?
    She died like this
    >   *Arms and legs are spread.*
    She's gonna wear her dresses up and down her knees.
    She's gonna choose her partner whoever he is.
    Hands up, Tootsie Lucy,
    >   *Hands are raised.*
    Hands down, Tootsie Lucy.
    >   *Hands are lowered.*
    I never went to college,
    I never went to school,
    But when I came back,
    I was an educated fool.[1]

5. Bathing beauty thinks she's cutey.
    If she jumps to twenty-four,
    She may have her turn once more.
    One, two, three, . . .
    >   *If the player is successful in jumping up to the count of twenty-four, she is given a second turn.*

---

1. The last four lines are appended to a great many rhymes, but they were not found to occur alone anywhere in the collection.

6. Black ants biting me,
   I can't get out.
   My mother called me,
   My sister called me,
   My brother called me,
   And I can't get out.

7. Blue bells, cockle shells[2]
   Evie, ivy, overhead.

8. Buster Brown, turn around,
   Buster Brown, touch the ground,
   Buster Brown, show your shoe,
   Buster Brown, how old are you?
   Are you one? Are you two? . . .
   > *The jumper runs out when he reaches his
   > age.*

9. Butterfly, butterfly, turn around,
   Butterfly, butterfly, touch the ground,
   Butterfly, butterfly, show your shoe,
   Butterfly, butterfly, that will do.

---

2. Variant: Blue berry, cocker cherry. This variant provides a good example of changing unfamiliar (and therefore nonsensical) words to something familiar.

10.   Charlie Chaplin went to France
       To teach the ladies how to dance;
       First the heel and then the toe,
       Round and round and out we go.

11.   Cinderella, dressed in yellow,
       Went upstairs[3] to see her fellow;
       On the way she met a snake.[4]
       How many kisses did he take?[5]
       One, two, three, . . .[6]
              Until the jumper misses.

12.   Donald Duck is a one-legged, one-legged duck,
       Donald Duck is a two-legged, two-legged duck,
       Donald Duck is a three-legged, three-legged
          duck . . .
              The count proceeds until the player misses.

13.   Down by the ocean, down by the sea,
       Johnny broke a milk bottle
       And blamed it on me.
       I told Ma, Ma told Pa,

---

   3. Variant: Went to the ball . . .
   4. Variant: Made a mistake and kissed a snake,
   5. Variant: How many doctors will it take?
   6. This rhyme was the one most commonly cited by informants under twenty. It also had the widest regional spread.

How many lickings did Johnny get?
One, two, three, . . .

14. Down in the meadow where the green grass grows,
There sat _____ as sweet as a rose.
Down came _____ and kissed her on the
    cheek.[7]
How many kisses did she get in a week?
One, two, three, . . .

15. Eenie, meenie, minie, moe
Crackie, feenie, finie, foe,
Uma, noochie, uppa, doochie,
Rick, bick, bango.

16. Fudge, fudge, county judge,
    _____ is gonna have a baby.
Wrap it up in toilet paper,
Send it up the elevator,
Boy, girl, twins, triplets,
Boy, girl, . . .
    Repeat until the jumper misses.

---

7. "Down in the Meadow" illustrates an effective means of teasing the jumper about her affection for some schoolmate, though sometimes the teasing is hurtful in that the second name may be some decidedly unattractive boy.

17.   Fudge, fudge, fudge,
      Kick a boom, boom,
      Calling on the judge, boom.
      Mama's got a new-born baby.
      It's a boy, boom!
      It's a girl, boom!
      Papa's going crazy!

18.   Fudge, fudge, tell the judge,
      Mama's got a brand new baby.
      Isn't a boy, isn't a girl,
      Just a plain old baby.
      Wrap it up in tissue paper,
      Send it down the elevator,
      First floor stop,
      Second floor stop,
      Third floor — throw it out the door.

19.   Gypsy, gypsy, please tell me
      What my husband's going to be.
      Rich man, poor man, beggar man, thief,
      Doctor, lawyer, Indian chief,
      (Tinker, tailor, cowboy, sailor.)

20.   H-E-L-P spells *help.*
      H is for high water.
                    The rope is swung high off the ground.

E is for eyes closed.
> *The jumper closes her eyes.*

L is for one leg.
> *The jumper hops on one foot.*

And *P* is for pepper.
> *The rope is swung very fast until the jumper misses.*

21. H-O-T spells *hot.*
> *The rope swingers call this out as they swing the rope slowly at first and build up to a fast speed.*

22. I like coffee, I like tea,
I'd like ＿＿＿＿＿＿ to jump in with me.
> *The person whose name is called will run in and join the jumper.*
> *Others may be added depending on the length of the rope.*

23. I love coffee, I love tea,
I love the boys, and they love me.
Yes, no, maybe so; yes, no, maybe so; . . .
> *The last line is repeated until the jumper misses.*

24.   I love coffee, I love tea,
      I love the boys and the boys love me.
      Tell your mama to keep her tongue;
      She had beaux when she was young.
      Tell your daddy the very same thing.
      He was the one who changed her name.

25.   I went upstairs to make my bed;
      I made a mistake and bumped my head.
      I said itchi, itchi, itchi, itchi,
      Itchi, itchi, itchi, itchi.
      I went upstairs to comb my hair;
      I made a mistake and combed my nose.
      I said itchi, . . .
              Lines three and four are a refrain.
      I went outside to milk the cow;
      I made a mistake and milked my ear.
      Itchi, . . .
      I went in the kitchen to bake a cake;
      I made a mistake and baked my bum.
      Itchi, . . .
      I went upstairs to find my shoe;
      I made a mistake and skinned my shin.
      Itchi, . . .
      I went outside to stop a fight;
      I made a mistake and started a fight.
      Itchi, . . .

26. Ice cream soda, ginger ale, pop.[8]
    Tell me the initial of your sweetheart.
    Is it A? B? C? . . .

    > *The jumper runs out on the appropriate letter.*

27. I'm a little Dutch girl dressed in blue
    And here are the things that I can do;
    Salute the captain, bow to the queen,
    And touch the bottom of a submarine.[9]

28. Jack and Jill were sitting in a tree
    K-I-S-S-I-N-G.
    First came a lover, then came marriage,
    Then came Jill with a baby carriage.
    One, two, three, . . .

29. Johnny over the ocean,
    Johnny over the sea,
    Johnny broke a bottle,
    And blamed it on me.
    I told Mama, Mama told Papa,
    Johnny got a whipping, H-O-T.[10]

---

8. Variant: Ice cream soda, cream on the top.
9. Variant: Salute the captain, curtsey to the queen, / And turn my back on the mean old king.
10. Variant: Johnny got a whipping, ha, ha, ha!

30.   Lady Bug, Lady Bug, turn around,
      Lady Bug, Lady Bug, touch the ground.

31.   Last night and the night before,
      Twenty-four robbers came
      Knocking at the door;
      I got up, let them in,[11]
      Hit them in the head
      With a rolling pin.
      Five, ten, fifteen, . . .

32.   London bridge is all broke down,
      All broke down, all broke down,
      London bridge is all broke down,
      My fair lady yours. Chip, chop,
      Chip, chop, cheese.

33.   Lula had a steamboat,
      Steamboat had a bell,
      Lula went to heaven,
      Steamboat went to hell –
      O, operator,
      Give me number nine:
      If she doesn't answer,

---

11. Variant: I went upstairs to get my gun, / You ought to see those robbers run.

Kick her be-
Hind the refrigerator,
I laid a piece of glass,
Lula slipped and fell
And cut her little a-a-a –
Ask me no questions,
Tell me no lies;
And this is the story
Of how Lula dies.

34. Mabel, Mabel, set the table,
Don't forget the red hot peas.[12]

35. Mama, Mama, I am sick,
Send for the doctor quick, quick, quick.
Doctor, Doctor, shall I die?
Yes, my child, but don't you cry.
How many pills shall I take?
One, two, three, . . .

36. Mary go round the sunshine,
Mary go round the moon,
Mary go round the sunshine,
Every afternoon.

---

12. Variant: Don't forget the salt, pepper, peas.

37.   Mary Mack all dressed in black,
       Twenty-four buttons down her back;
       She asked her ma for fifteen cents,
       To see the elephant jump the fence.
       He jumped so high he touched the sky,
       He never came back till the fourth of July.

38.   Mother, Mother, I am sick;
       Call the doctor double quick.
       In came the doctor,
       In came the nurse,
       In came the lady with the alligator purse.
       Out went the doctor,
       Out went the nurse,
       Out went the lady with the alligator purse.
              Three players may run in and out at the ap-
              propriate time.

39.   My mama she told me to open the door,
       But I didn't wanna.
       I opened the door
       And he fell on the floor,
       That crazy old man from China!
       My mama she told me to take off his hat,
       But I didn't wanna.
       I took off his hat
       And he smelled like a rat,

That crazy old man from China!
My mama she told me to take off his coat
But I didn't wanna.
I took off his coat
And he smelled like a goat,
That crazy old man from China!
My mama she told me to get him a drink,
But I didn't wanna.
I got him a drink
And he ate up the sink,
That crazy old man from China!
My mama she told me to put him to bed,
But I didn't wanna.
I put him to bed
And he fell on his head,
That crazy old man from China!
My mama she told me to bury him deep,
But I didn't wanna.
I buried him deep
And he stuck out his feet,
That crazy old man from China!

40. My mommy had a baby,
     She named him Tiny Tim.
     She put him in the bathtub
     To see if he could swim.
     He drank up all the water

And ate up all the soap;
But it wouldn't go down his throat. [13]
My mother called the doctor,
My mother called the doctor,
The doctor called the nurse,
The nurse called the lady with the alligator purse.
The doctor said, "The measles,"
The nurse said, "The mumps."
The lady with the alligator purse said, "Cock-a-
   doodle-doo." [14]

41.   My mother is from England,
My father is from France;
My boyfriend came from the USA
With a hole in the seat of his pants.
He gave me all his peaches,
He gave me all his pears,
He gave me all his fifty cents
And kissed me on the stairs.
I gave him back his peaches,
I gave him back his pears,
I gave him back his fifty cents
And kicked him down the stairs.

---

13. Variant: Then he went to bed / With a bubble in his throat.
14. Variant: I don't need the doctor, / I don't need the nurse, / I don't need the lady with the alligator purse.

42. North, South, East, West,
        *The jumper must turn in the proper direction
        while she is jumping.*
        _____ is the one who is the best.
        The jumper names her successor.
     One, two, three, . . .
        Until jumper misses.

43. Not last night, but the night before,
     Twenty-four robbers came knocking at my door.
     As they ran in, I ran out;
     This is the song I began to shout.
     Spanish dancers, turn around,
     Spanish dancers, touch the ground,
     Spanish dancers, run out of town.

44. One cold night when we were all in bed,
     Pa left the lantern burning in the shed,[15]
     Cow kicked it over and this is what she said,
     "There'll be a hot time in the old town tonight."

45. One little, two little, three little Indians,
     Four little, five little, six little Indians,
     Seven little, eight little, nine little Indians,
     Ten little Indians in the pawpaw patch,

---

15. Variant: Old Mother Hubbard put the lantern in the shed.

Come on, girls, let's go find them,
> *The above line may be repeated three or
> more times.*

Way down yonder in the pawpaw patch.

46.   One, two, hallelujah,
Three, four, God bless you,[16]
Five, six, pick up sticks,
Seven, eight, lay them straight,
Nine, ten, a big fat hen.[17]

47.   One, two, three, four, five, six, seven.
All good children go to heaven.
All the rest go down below
Where the bad man lives, you know.

48.   One, two, three, Salima,[18]
Four, five, six, Salima,
Seven, eight, nine, Salima,
Ten, Salima, H-O-T!

---

16. Variant: Three, four, helleluja, / Five, six, hallelujah.

17. The reader has no doubt noticed that many rhymes throughout the collection appear in whole or in part in other collections as "nursery rhymes." Often the adaptations provide interesting sidelights on social changes.

18. I have been unable to find a source for *Salima.* The rhyme came from a group of black school children, and none of them knew what it meant. One possibility is the biblical character Salome, daughter of the infamous Herodias, who had the head of John the Baptist brought on a salver into the banquet room.

49. Postman, postman, do your duty,
    Here comes a lady with American beauty.
    She can wiggle, she can wobble,
    She can do the split.
    She can wear her dresses up above the knees,
    She never went to college,
    She never went to school,
    But when she came back
    She was an educated fool.

50. Rin Tin Tin swallowed a pin;
    Went to the doctor, but the doctor wasn't in.
    In came the doctor, in came the nurse,
    In came the lady with the alligator purse.
    Mother, mother, will I die?
    Yes, my son, but don't you cry.

51. Roses are red
    Violets are blue;
    If you can jump to a hundred,
    I can too.

52. Rumble, rumble in the pot,
    Take one out and leave it hot.

53. Salt and pepper were a pair of roans.
    Drove 'em to town and they jiggled my bones.
    One, two, three. . . .

54. Salt, pepper, vinegar, mustard,
    Hot, H-O-T!

55. Same song, second verse,
    Couldn't be better,
    So it's got to be worse.

    > *The above was chanted at the end of any rhyme to lengthen the jumping period.*

56. Sweet potatoes, okra, tomatoes, peas,
    Your mama says you gotta eat a lot of these;
    Macaroni, alphabets, all in a group,
    Then you put 'em in a bowl and call it Campbell's soup.
    How many vegetables can you eat?
    One, two, three, . . .

57. Teddy Bear, Teddy Bear, touch your nose,
    Teddy Bear, Teddy Bear, touch your toes,
    Teddy Bear, Teddy Bear, touch the ground,
    Teddy Bear, Teddy Bear, turn around.
    Teddy Bear, Teddy Bear, throw a kiss,
    Teddy Bear, Teddy Bear, get out before you miss.

Teddy Bear, Teddy Bear, go upstairs,
Teddy Bear, Teddy Bear, say your prayers
Teddy Bear, Teddy Bear, sell your biscuits,[19]
Teddy Bear, Teddy Bear, how many biscuits have
    you sold?
One, two, three, . . .

58.   Texaco, Texaco, over the hill in Mexico,
      Do the split, split,
      Give a high kick, kick,
      Turn around, round,
      Get out of town.
      Please come back, back,
      Sit on a tack, tack,
      Brush your hair, hair,
      We're all through with you, you,
      So go, go, go, and don't come back.

59.   Two, four, six, eight,
      Johnny found a rattlesnake,
      Snake died, Johnny cried,
      Two, four, six, eight.

---

19. Variant: Teddy Bear, Teddy Bear, turn off the light, / Teddy Bear, Teddy Bear, say goodnight.

60. Up the ladder, down the ladder,
     A-B-C.
     Down the ladder, up the ladder,
     H-O-T.

61. Virginia had a baby, his name was Tiny Tim,
     She put him in the bathtub to teach him how to swim.
     He swam up the lake,
     He swam down the lake,
     Now Virginia's baby has a stomach ache.

62. Was an old man named Michael Finnegan,
     Long beard grew out of his chinnegan,
     Along came a wind and blew it in again.
     Poor old Michael Finnegan,
     Again! Again!
              *The last line is a call to go through the rhyme
              again.*

63. Way down South where bananas grow,
     An ant stepped on an elephant's toe,
     The elephant cried with tears in his eyes,
     Why don't you pick on someone your size?

64. Went down the road,
     The road was muddy.
     Stumped my toe,
     My toe was bloody.

How many times did I stump my toe?
One, two, three, . . .

65. Went to visit Grandpa's farm,
Billy goat chased me around the barn.
Chased me up an apple tree,
This is what he said to me:
I love coffee, I love tea,
I love _____ and _____ loves me.

66. Your eyes may shine
And your teeth may grit,
But what you see
Is what you get.
    Repeat faster.

3
AUTOGRAPHS

*"As sure as the grass grows
round the stump,
You are my darling sugar
lump."*

THE ORIGIN OF AUTOGRAPHS IS LOST IN HISTORY, though their provenance may be traced to such sources as the seventeenth-century practice of passing favorite poems among the courtiers. Centuries before that, however, royal patronage of fawning poets had set the stage for the modern autograph. ("Autograph" here does not refer to that current use of the word, especially as used by girls in their teens or older, which requires only a signature, usually limited to those of artists, particularly literary or dramatic artists of note, as well as those of sportsmen and others who have caught the fancy of the public.)

Only rarely do adults keep autograph books in the present times, though I have in my files one group of verses of serious tone and some elegance of style collected by a college student in the forties. It contains many entries that have flowery lines interspersed with lines from nineteenth-century British poetry. Typically, however, the autograph in recent decades is compiled by children in the fourth, fifth, and sixth grades. The arrival and disappearance at school of the little books follow the same mysterious pattern of jacks and marbles—games that children play feverishly for a few weeks and drop as quickly with no apparent planning or notice. Like the robin, whose flights are meticulously recorded though little understood, these games are also harbingers of spring.

The standard autograph book is a small album roughly six

43

inches in width and four inches in height and has pastel-colored pages—green, blue, yellow, pink. It is most often poorly constructed of sleazy paper, though it may have a richly embossed cover. It rarely survives a season of being passed around among friends, but if it does it may find its way into a drawer or chest to be forgotten for years. Eventually, it will be found and either become a prized possession of sentimental worth or tossed into a trash basket.

Typical also is the peculiar way of turning down the pages. No one seems to know why, though the practical person may offer the most obvious reason: it makes turning the pages simple. The folds are made by making a four-inch diagonal, using the height of the page as a gauge. The folds alternate: the first is folded toward the top of the page and the next toward the bottom.

Like jump-rope rhymes, the verses reflect the interests of the collector. Many show a developing interest in the opposite sex; and although boys typically have not had autograph books of the kind described above, they have often written in them. One interesting group of verses represents a trend toward creativity in the complimentary close. The businesslike "Yours truly" gives way to "Yours till butter flies" and other simple word play. Such closes flourished during a period in the thirties and then died out much as did the "moron jokes" of the fifties.

One custom seemed to be followed only in one geographical region of the state and among members of a minority group. At the end of the autograph, a separate message was likely to appear: "Kard me, kid" or "Card me at your leisure." The contributor interpreted the message as an invitation to keep in touch.

The autographs fall neatly into three categories: those which have a serious tone, those which are playful, and those which have a clever visual contrivance of some kind. The "trick" may be in using rebus-like symbols or in placing the words on the page in a nonstandard fashion.

The most enduring autograph is "Roses Are Red," but its popularity may lie in the ease with which one can parody the simple two-beat lines with the second and fourth lines rhyming. Almost as popular is the verse beginning "When you get married . . . ." The gist of the verse, no doubt devastatingly funny to youngsters, invariably takes on the characteristic humor of a comic strip. The high number of variants for these two autographs made it necessary to select several representative rhymes in each category.

Finally, something must be said about the appearance in the forties and fifties of the "slam book." Finding one was difficult. The slam book, unlike the autograph book, was a homemade contrivance of pages from a notebook held together in a variety of ways. The one passed on to me by its owner was simply three-hole theme paper clamped in a green research paper cover. Typically, the first page contained the signatures of the persons invited to write in the book, usually the members of the class. However, the information sought by the owner was potentially so ravaging that teachers often forbade slam books (an act that assured instant popularity) and confiscated them if they found them. The obvious result is that slam books went underground—one reason, I suspect, that nearly every person in grades four to six in the late forties and early fifties, when slam books were in their heydey, remembers them but has lost her own book.

The organization of the slam book may vary slightly, but a common procedure was to assign a question to a page and then have each child in the order established on the first page write an answer. The importance of the matter is that the answer had to be "honest." Questions ranged from "Do you play in the band?" to "Who is the ugliest girl in the class?" A contributor stated to me that she cried for days when she found out her "very best friend" did not name her the most popular girl in the class. The psychological forces making the pastime attractive enough to expose oneself to such pain must indeed be complex. Slam books are, it seems, the dark side of the ubiquitous autograph books, and in the appropriate hands would probably reveal much that we do not yet know about child motivation.

Although the slam book is a part of child lore, it was excluded from this collection both because there was a dearth of material and because the language was not rote.

Section A

1.   A crust of bread and a corner to live in,
     A minute to smile and an hour to weep in,
     A pint of joy to a peck of troubles.
     Never a laugh, but the moans come double —
        And that is life!

2.   A friend is a present you give yourself,
     That is one of the old-time songs.
     So I put you down with the best of them,
     For you are where the best belong.

3.   Always bear this in mind,
     True friends are hard to find.
     When you find one good and true,
     Don't forsake the old for the new.

4.   Always remember
     And never forget,
     That brown-eyed girl
     That loves you yet.

5.   As sure as a vine grows round the stump,
     You are my darling sugar lump.

6.   Deep hidden, like forget-me-nots
     In shady garden ways,

My wishes blossom on each page
That opens to your gaze.
But you will see between the lines
The heart's forget-me-nots,
That whisper to you,
"Remember me" and says
You're not forgot.

7.   Do all the good you can
To all the people you can
In every way you can
As long as ever you can.

8.   Do all the good you can for the worst of us,
And all the evil you can for the best of us,
Then everything will be all right for the rest of us.

9.   Down in the meadow
Carved in a rock,
Three little words:
Forget me not.

10.   Fortunate is he who may see the experience of
another,
Learn from it, profit from it,
Without paying all the price for it.

11. Four things a man must learn to do
     If he will make his record true.
     To think without confusion clearly,
     To love his fellow man sincerely,
     To act from honest motives purely,
     And trust in God and heaven securely.

12. Gold is like love,
     Hard to get and hard to hold,
     Some are happy,
     And some are blue,
     But I will never be happy
     Until I hold you in my arms.

13. He who says that I have not fought a good fight and
         won,
     Reject my outstretched hand.

14. High on a mountain
     Engraved in a rock
     Are three little words:
     Forget-me-not.

15. If a task is once begun
     Never leave it till it's done.
     Be the labor great or small
     Do it well or not at all.

16. If you cannot do great things,
     Do the small things in a great way.

17. If you have tried and have not won,
     Never stop for crying;
     For all that is great and good is done
     Just by patient trying.

18. In this little advice let my words
         ring as an echo:
     Remember that self-praise is a
         dangerous weapon.

19. It's a pleasure to meet you
     And a pain to part,
     But remember you will always
     Have my heart.

20. May all your cheers
     Throughout the years
     Be filled with fun and laughter.
     And this, my dear,
     May God hear
     And grant to you ever after.

21. May the light before you be bright and clear,
     And lead you to bright and happy years.

22. May this life bring you all the happiness you can
    stand
    And only enough sorrow to show you the difference.

23. New occasions teach new duties,
    Time makes ancient good uncouth.
    They must upward still and onward
    Who should keep abreast of truth.

24. One tale is enough
    Until another is told.

25. Remember me by the moon that shines at night;
    Remember me by the sun that shines by day;
    Remember me, and don't forget to write.

26. Remember me while life is sweet,
    Remember me until next we meet,
    And if the grave should be my bed,
    Remember me when I am dead.

27. Remember that you will always be regarded
    As a link in my chain of memories.

28.   Remember well and bear in mind
      That a constant friend is hard to find.
      But when you find one kind and true,
      Do not trade the old for the new.

29.   Roses are red,
      Violets are blue;
      Angels in Heaven
      Know I love you.

30.   She is the dearest pal I know;
      Someone to go with me wherever I go
      Or direct me when I am wrong;
      There's so much in her I know I couldn't have
          known,
      Oh, what a sweet world there would be,
      If everyone understood like my pal and me.
      No wars, hating or confusion would we have,
      If everybody agreed like me and my pal.

31.   Some may wish you fortune,
      Some may wish you fame,
      But I wish you, _____ , dear,
      A spotless Christian name.

32.   Success is failure turned inside out,
          The silver lining of clouds of doubt,

And you never can tell how close you are;
  It may be near when it seems so far.
So stick to the fight when you're hardest hit;
  It is when things seem worst that we must not quit.

33. The man who sits and waits
      For good to come along
   Isn't worth the breath it takes
      To tell him he is wrong.

34. There are loyal hearts, spirits brave,
   Souls that are pure and true.
   Then give to the world the best you have
   And the best will come back to you.

35. There are three ships:
   Silver ship, gold ship,
   But the most valuable ship is friendship.

36. Thou must be true thyself
   If thou the truth wouldst teach;
   Thy soul must overflow,
   If thou another's soul wouldst reach;
   It needs the overflow of heart
   To give the lips full speech.

37. True friends are like diamonds,
     Precious and rare.
     False friends are like autumn leaves
     Scattered everywhere.

38. We cannot change yesterday, that is clear;
     We cannot change tomorrow until it is here;
     So the best thing for you and me
     Is to make today as happy as can be.

39. What shall I write?
     What shall it be?
     Just two little words,
     Remember me.

40. When days and months have glided by
     And through this book I cast my eye,
     I shall remember it was friends sincere
     Who left these small remembrances here.
             *The above lines were often written by the
             owner of the autograph book on the inside
             front cover.*

41. When evening pulls the curtain to
     And pins it with a star,
     Remember you always have a friend
     No matter where you are.

42. When I first saw you
     And heard your sweet voice,
     I set aside all other girls
     And took you as my choice.

43. When on this page you chance to look,
     Just think of me and close the book.
     I write these simple lines for thee,
     Whene'er you see them, think of me.

44. When the golden sun is sinking
     And your path is no more trod,
     May your name in gold be written
     In the autograph of God.

45. When the great Scorer comes
     To write against your name,
     He writes not whether you won or lost,
     But how you played the game.

46. When the rose on your cheek has faded
     And your hair is turning grey,
     May you be the sweet old lady
     As the girl you are today.

47. While on this earth of sorrow and tears,
    I may be needed in future years;
    Wherever I go I'll be your friend,
    Prove true to you to the end.

48. With the ropes of the past
    You can ring the bells of the future.

Section B

1. _____, _____, don't be blue,
   Frankenstein was ugly too.

2. _____ and _____ sitting in a tree,
   K-I-S-S-I-N-G.
   First comes love, then comes marriage,
   Then comes _____ with a baby carriage.

3. _____ and _____ went for a ride,
   _____ fell out and _____ cried,
   We'll get married
   In half a year!

4. _____ had a little car,
   And it was painted red,
   And everywhere that _____ went,
   The cops picked up the dead.

5. _____ is her name,
_____ is her station;
Leave her alone, boys,
Till she gets her education.

> *In these and the blanks in the following group, supply the appropriate first and last names of the girl and/or boy.*

6. _____ is sweet,
_____ is mean,
_____ is sweet
Like a sweet sixteen.

7. _____ now, _____ forever,
_____ now, but not forever.

8. _____ the fair,
_____ the lovable,
_____ the lily maid
Of _____ Street.

9. *A* is for apple,
P is for plum,
Y is for every
yum, yum, yum.

10. Apples on the table,
    Peaches on the shelf,
    I'm getting tired
    Of sleeping by myself.

11. As green as grass,
    As round as a stump,
    You are my darling
    Sugar lump.

12. Ashes to ashes,
    Dust to dust,
    You're one friend[1]
    That I can trust.

13. Blue as the Gates of Heaven,
    Green as the Gates of Hell,
    Durn the boy who'll kiss a girl
    And then go off and tell.

14. Boys come, boys go,
    Boys are the ones in the know;
    They think they'll tell everyone
    _____ is the "swinging" one.

---

1. Variant: If God won't have you, / The devil must.

15. Boys' love is just like snuff,
    One dip and that's enough;
    Girls' love is just like gold,
    Hard to get and hard to hold.

16. Can't think — too dumb,
    Inspiration — won't come,
    Can't write — bum pen,[2]
    Good luck — Amen!

17. Don't make love by the garden;
    The bugs may be blind, but the neighbors aren't.

18. Don't tell a secret by a garden gate,
    Flowers are deaf, but the neighbors ain't.

19. Don't worry if your job is small
    And your rewards are few;
    Remember that the mighty oak
    Was once a nut like you.

20. Down in the meadow
    Carved in a rock,
    Three little words—
    Forget me not.

---

2. Variant: Bad lead—worse pen, / Best wishes—Amen.

21. Fire is red,
    Water is blue,
    But flirty little girls
    Remind me of you.

22. God made bushes,
    God made trees,
    God made _____
    For boys to squeeze.

23. Good luck for you at ninety-two,
    Even though I cry and say boo-hoo.

24. He sat on your doorstep,
    Your lips he gently pressed,
    Your father gave the sign
    And the bulldog did the rest.

25. Here's hoping that in the years to come,
    We won't be finding _____ standing over a
        hot stove
    Crying in a frying pan,
    Just for the sake of pleasing a man.

26. I am a mean old lady;
    Would you be my matey?

27. I love you, I love you,
     I love you divine.
     Please give me your bubble gum,
     You're sitting on mine.

28. I love you, I love you,
     I love you, I do;
     But don't get excited,
     I love monkeys too.

29. I love you little,
     I love you big,
     I love you like
     A little pig.

30. I love you once,
     I love you twice,
     I love you next to Jesus Christ.

31. I met you, I bet you,
     I'll never forget you.

32. I ought'o cry,
     I ought'o laugh
     I ought'o sign
     Your autograph.

33.   I thought and thought
      And thought in vain;
      At last I thought
      I'd sign my name.

34.   I wish I were a grapefruit,
      I'll tell you the reason why;
      If you didn't like me,
      I'd squirt you in the eye.

35.   I wish you luck, I wish you joy,
      I wish you first a baby boy;
      And when his hair begins to curl,
      I wish you then a baby girl.
      And when her hair is up in pins,[3]
      I wish you then a set of twins.

36.   If all the boys lived across the sea,
      What a good swimmer you would be.

37.   If all the boys were across the lake,
      What a good swimmer _____ would make.

---

   3. Variant: And when they're through with safety pins, / I wish you then
a pair of twins.

38. If you go to Heaven before I do,
    Punch a little hole, and pull me through.

39. If you love _____ like I do,
    There will be a wedding in a year or two.

40. I'll write in pink,
    Because you stink.

41. I'm not a fish,
    But drop me a line.

42. I'm too young to wear Kickies,
    I'm too young to wear blue,
    I'm too young to be married,
    But I'm not too young to love you.

43. It tickles me pink,
    It makes me laugh,
    To think you want
    My autograph.

44. I've never been to college,
    I've never been to school,
    But when it comes to loving,
    I'm an educated fool.

45. Little girl, little girl,
    Don't you cry.
    You'll be a big girl
    By and by.

46. Long may you live,
    Long may you tarry,
    Court who you please,
    But mind who you marry.

47. Love is a plaything
    Love is a toy,
    If you want your heart broken,
    Give it to a boy.

48. Love is like a lump of gold;
    Hard to get and hard to hold.

49. Love many, hate few,
    Always paddle your own canoe.

50. Mary had a little lamb,
    She gave him castor oil,
    He jumped across the fence one day,
    And fertilized the soil.

51. Many now,
    Many forever,
    Do now
    But not forever.

52. May all your troubles be little ones.

53. My father owns the butcher shop,
    My mother cuts the meat,
    And I'm the little hot dog
    That runs around the street.

54. Nasturtiums by another name
    Would just as sweetly smell;
    In addition, they might be
    Easier to spell.

55. Peaches grow in California and in Florida too;
    But it takes a state like Mississippi
    To grow as fine a peach as you.

56. Poor little _____
    Sitting on a fence,
    Trying to make a dollar
    Out of ninety-nine cents.

57.   Posies are pink,
      Daisies are yellow,
      If I were eleven
      I'd be your fellow.

58.   Remember:
      Always be natural,
      Always be true,
      Always paddle your own canoe.

59.   Remember —
      Never let a kiss fool you
      And never let a fool kiss you.

60.   Remember, dear, and bear in mind,
      A good-looking man is hard to find,
      So when you find one old and grey,
      Hold to his coat tail night and day.
      For a hoop on a barrel is sure to rust,
      And a good-looking man is hard to trust.

61.   Remember Grant,
      Remember Lee,
      The heck with them,
      Remember me.

62. Remember the North,
Remember the South,
Remember me
And my big mouth!

63. Remember well and bear in mind,
A true friend is hard to find;
And when you find one good and true,
Change not the old for the new.

64. Roses are red,
Violets are blue,
Sugar is sweet,
And so are you.

65. Roses are red,
Onions are green,
Your legs are pretty,
As far as I've seen.

66. Roses are red,
Violets are green,
You've got a shape
Like a B17.

67.   Roses are red,
      Violets are blue,
      I love ——————,
      And I hate you.

68.   Roses are red,
      Violets are blue,
      The sidewalk is cracked
      And so are you.

69.   Roses are red,
      Violets are blue,
      God made me pretty,
      But why aren't you?

70.   Roses are red,
      Violets are blue,
      No knife shall cut
      Our love in two.

71.   Roses are red,
      Violets are black,
      You'd look better
      With a knife in your back.

72. Roses are red,
    Violets are blue,
    Monkeys like you
    Should be in the zoo.

73. Roses on my shoulders,
    Slippers on my feet,
    I'm Daddy's little darling.
    Don't you think I'm sweet?

74. Save up your pennies,
    Until you get a dime,
    Then come up
    To see me some time.

75. Snow is white,
    And so is flour.
    I think of _____
    Hour by hour.

76. Sweet sixteen, Mother's pet.
    Never been kissed by the right boy yet.

77. The little gray elephant sat on the grass.
    The little gray elephant sat on his —
    Don't get nervous, don't get alarmed.
    The little gray elephant sat on his arm.

78. The river is wide
    And you can't step it.
    I love you,
    And I can't help it.

79. The stork flew north,
    The stork flew south,
    With little _____ in his mouth;
    When he found she was a nut,
    He dropped her in the _____'s hut.

80. Think of me now.
    Think of me then.
    Think of me as _____'s girlfriend.

81. This is for dirty people only:
    S O A P

82. This page is yellow,
    So is cheese.
    You're the kind
    To hug and squeeze!
    > *To be written on a yellow page in the auto-
    > graph book.*

83. To miss a kiss is simply awful,
    To miss a kiss is awfully simple,
    Kisses spread germs I've heard it stated,
    Kiss me, baby, I'm vaccinated.

84. Too much moonlight,
    Too many kisses,[4]
    Two weeks later
    You're Mr. and Mrs.

85. Up the hickory,
    Down the pine,
    God bless you, honey,
    I wish you were mine.

86. What! Write in your book!
    Where the learned may look!
    Where the critic may spy!
    No! Never! Not I!

87. When you are ashamed
    And your face turns red,
    Count the cooties
    That crawl on your head.

---

4. Variant: Two little cars, / Two little kisses.

88.   When you are grown
         And want to marry a fool,
         Marry a boy from ＿＿＿＿＿＿ high school.

89.   When you are married,
         And down on your knees,
         Think of me — single —
         And doing as I please.

90.   When you are married,
         And have twenty-five;
         Don't call it a family,
         Call it a tribe.

91.   When you get married
         And live in Japan,
         Send me a kiss
         On an old tin can.

92.   When you get married
         And live in a shack,
         Teach your children
         To spit through a crack.

93. When you get married
    And live in Spain,
    Come and see me
    On the choo-choo train.

94. When you get married
    And live in a truck,
    Order your children
    From Sears and Roebuck.

95. When you get old
    And out of shape,
    Go buy you a girdle
    For two ninety-eight.

96. When you get married
    And live on a hill,
    Name your little boy
    Buffalo Bill.

97. When you get married
    And live on a hill,
    Send me a kiss
    By a whippoorwill.

98. When you get married
    And your husband gets cross,
    Pick up a broom
    And show him who's boss.

99. When you get old
    And can hardly see,
    Put on your specs
    And think of me.

100. When you get old
     And think you're sweet,
     Pull off your shoes
     And smell your feet.

101. When you are swimming and about to drown,
     Think of me and then go down!

102. When you buy a house,
     Don't allow rats;
     Have a lot of everything,
     Except a lot of brats.

103. You are a cute little girl
     With a cute little figure.
     Keep the boys away
     Until you get a little bigger.

104.   You are crazy,
       You are nuts.
       Happy little moron,
       Putt, putt, putt.

105.   You can fall from a mountain,
       You can fall from above,
       But the best way to fall
       Is to fall in love.

106.   Your head is like a ball of straw;
       Your nose is long and funny;
       Your mouth is like a cellar door,
       But I still love you, honey.

107.   You're not a Northern beauty,[5]
       You're not a Southern rose,
       You're just a little schoolgirl,
       With freckles on your nose.

---

5. Variant: You're not a bathing beauty.

Section C

1. A road to love,
    A road to success,
    I know you'll love
    This road until you die.
    I love you, oh, yes.
    > *Written between curved lines to represent a road.*

2. All nuts look in this corner.
    > *Written diagonally high in the right-hand corner.*

3. Around this page I've searched a lot,
    To find a little empty spot
    To plant this sweet forget-me-not.
    > *Written in a circle with a flower in the center.*

4. | Be good | as a Christian |
    | Wise | as a saint |
    | And | if a boy asks you to |
    | Kiss | him, tell |
    | Him | you can't. |

    > *To be read across the line in the normal way and then down the first column.*

5. By hook, by crook,
   I will be the last
   To write in this book.
   > *To be written on the inside of the back cover.*

6. Dot.
   Blot ●
   Forget me not.

7. G. I. Haircut,
   G. I. Hat,
   G. I. This and
   G. I. That.
   G. I. Love you,
   G. I. Do.
   G. I. Hope you love me too.

8. I know that you have many friends, 'tis true,
   So many that this book will be packed.
   So to give them plenty of room,
   I'm waiting for you in the back.
   > *Written on the last page.*

9. I wrote all the way down this page to say "Hi!"
   > *Written diagonally from the upper left corner*
   > *of the page to the lower right corner.*

10. I've come all the way down this hill
    To tell you I love you still.
          Written as Example 9.

11.
Read	see	that	me?
up	will	I	love
and	you	love	you
down	and	you.	Do

    To be read down the first column, up the second, etc.

12. Remember M
    Remember E
    Put them together
    And remember me

13. Remember the girl from the city,
    Remember the girl from the town,
    Remember the girl who ruined your book
    By writing upside down.
          To be written upside down on the page.

14. Some people are dumb and write up and down,
    But I am smart and write all around.
          To be written in one line to form a circle.

15.   To save some room for you and your lover
      Poor little me had to write on the cover.

16.   2 sweet
      2 be
      4 gotten
      2 nice
      2 be
      8 up

17.   U
      R
      2 young to go with boys

18.   U are
      2 sweet
      4 me

19.   U R   2 young   2 young
        +   2 go   +   2 marry
            4 boys   4 awhile

20. When you get old
    And live in hedges,
    Remember who
    Writes around edges.

    > *The first line is written at the top of the page,
    > the second down the right margin, the third
    > at the bottom, and the fourth up the left
    > margin.*

21. When you're out in the country
    And see a lot of hedges,
    Remember the girl
    Who wrote around the edges.

    > *Same as above.*

22. YY U V
    YY U B
    IC U R
    YY 4 me

    > *YY should be pronounced 2 Y's*

4

TAUNTS, JEERS, & OTHER MISCELLANY

Liar! Liar! Pants afire!

ALTHOUGH THEY WEAR the protective clothing of innocence, children are often barbarous and insensitive. Most of the first eighteen or twenty years of their lives are spent undergoing a rigorous training period during which the institutions given to such matters (in the United States the home, church, and school—but probably not in that order) apply themselves with varying degrees of success to dislodge the child from his self-appointed position in the center of the world, a position he has assumed to be absolute.

During the process, children cope with adults as best they can, compromising now and then, sometimes yielding ostensibly, sometimes in actuality. With their peers, however, there is no such illusionary behavior. They fight for their "territory" any way they can. One way is to belittle their playmates. A whole repertoire of rhymes and jingles, chanted with the intent of inflicting discomfort on the adversary, has sprung up. The custom of taunts, however, can stake no claim to originality, for even the Old Testament Jews knew the acute prick of derision: in the Revised Standard Version of the Bible one finds in Micah 2:4 "In that day they shall take up a taunt song against you." Also, the *brag* of Beowulf, the *gab* of Charlemagne's nephew Roland, as well as many songs of Indian tribes, all intended to make the enemy fearful and therefore vulnerable point up the psychological advantage of winning ritualistically even before the fray begins. The modern American "pep rally" provides an obvious example, with play supplanting reality.

It is small wonder that if adults find psychological satisfaction in magnifying their own courage by deriding the enemy, children perform the same exercise. The child is still exploring his own environment. He is less sure than he needs to be who are his friends and who are his enemies; in childhood there is little understanding of the qualities separating the two. The lines are tenuous ones, and today's friends may become tomorrow's enemies. Taunts and jeers, therefore, become less threatening—a kind of derision that may be taken as a joke if one chooses. Even the most reticent of youngsters may feel totally secure in the knowledge that "my daddy is better (stronger, more handsome, and so forth) than yours."

Little has been written about one aspect of teasing: the adult, usually a parent or other relative, sometimes takes pleasure in tormenting the child. The result is not often altogether unpleasant, for many children return over and over to have the same tricks played on them. While still a child small enough to get sticky fingers when gooey desserts were served, I was told by an uncle that when I ate such foods they ran out behind the knees and made the skin there sticky. Lo, it was always so, and the laughter from the rest of the family did not override the pleasure of being the center of attention when I felt behind my knees. The same relative assured me that if I wished to be a boy I should kiss my elbow and the metamorphosis would take place immediately. I spent many unsuccessful hours testing the theory.

One other example will suffice. Parents have a mysterious way of knowing a good deal more about the child than he suspects. The wise parent of my generation never let the questioning child know the source of his information, though the evidence of guilt was often as obvious as the cake icing on the child's face. The parent commonly answered, when asked who "snitched," "A little bird told me." For a bird that I never saw, it remained eerily close by throughout my childhood.

It is perhaps to be expected that taunts cluster in those areas where a child is likely to be most insecure. School and playground are obvious places. Some rhymes, however, are saucy for their own sakes. Children simply enjoy being impertinent, and they are likely to be immune from rebuke if their taunts are ritualized. For example, the subject of underwear turns into ribaldry, especially if the underclothing happens to show when children are playing. A good deal of activity in play tends to coincide with the budding interest in details of sexual behavior; and since most children, even in a sex-oriented society, still get their education from their peers where ignorance is pooled on the streets and school grounds, they tend to hide their embarrassment behind raucous joking and teasing. This situation accounts for the large number of taunts that make reference to underwear.

If a girl's slip shows, "Cotton's low" or "Pinky's slipping" or "White, white, getting married tonight." An interesting discrimination between the hem and shoulder strap showing is made by "It's snowing up North" and "It's snowing down South." If an older female's panties or girdle shows, then "She took my picture."

Another significant group of rhymes pertains to food. At summer camps and other informal gatherings where children are not closely supervised, there has grown up a group of verses which parody the Christian grace, or thanks, given at the table before eating. And since the thanksgiving is an open testimony in those homes where it is used, any parody is a sacrilege and therefore taboo. Typical of them is

> Good food, good meat,
> Good God, let's eat.

Nor should it come as a surprise that a great many of these parodies are earthy and therefore doubly taboo:

> Peas, beans, they're good for the heart,
> The more you eat, the more you _____.

Most children not only know the rhyme above, but its variant as well:

> Peas, beans, the musical fruit,
> The more you eat, the more you _____.

The preteen rebels stoutly against the niceties of table etiquette. He may be forced to observe a certain decorum under the eyes of parents and teachers, but elsewhere he takes pleasure in his ability to nauseate his audience, which almost invariably includes young squealing females. A typical recitation might be as follows:

Fifteen miles of greasy, grimy, gopher guts, chopped up chicken feet, mutilated monkey meat, French-fried eyeballs soaked in poodle blood, and I forgot my spoon. Please pass the ketchup.

The lines strongly suggest that children get pleasure from language play for its own sake. The heavy alliteration is an obvious factor. Rhymed name calling is also common. "Howard is a coward," "Ella (pronounced Eller) has a feller," and "Myrtle has a turtle up her girdle" are typical of a long list. A child, usually with an appreciative audience of one or more children, asks another to pronounce m-u-l-y, r-u-l-y, d-u-l-y, and finally J-u-l-y. The victim of the prank will almost invariably mispronounce the name of the month, providing much hilarity at his expense. Or the child will be told to say: "He chewed and chewed until his jaws dropped down." He is instructed to go at an increasing rate of speed. At some point he will anticipate the two *d*'s at the end and say: "He chewed and chewed until his *drawers* dropped down." An adult is hard put to recall the flavor of the ensuing merriment.

As the short discussion above indicates, taunts and jeers come in a wide variety of forms. None of them is a basic part of a game, but they are often recited during the playing of games and they have become ritualized to the extent that it is fairly predictable where and under what conditions they will occur. They also range widely in the sharpness of the barb, the first group involving parent-child play being totally innocuous. In fact, the semantic content of each rhyme is a fairly clear indication of the relationship between the taunter and the taunted. It was on this basis that the collection in this section was divided from mild parent-child relationships to teacher-child and child-child ridicule, the last being by far the most prolific as well as most acute.

The rhymes included in this last section in no way exhaust the potential list. Limitations of space made strict selection necessary. Little mention has been made of games that carry their own ritualistic language, often a song, as in a "round game" appropriate for small children. A common type is "Ring Around the Rosie" where children move around in a circle until they are told by the song to squat on the last line. Superstitions, too, are prevalent among children. They avoid stepping on a crack on a cement sidewalk, for "Step on a crack and / You'll break your mother's back." An interesting variant has "break your sister's [i.e., nun's] back." Children are wary of worms: "If you see a thousand-leg worm, close your mouth; because if he counts your teeth, you'll die." And if one's nose itches, the child explains it as a sign: "I smell peaches, my nose itches / Somebody's coming with a hole in his britches."

An entire book could be written on parodies that children (and adults) concoct. Only a few that were particularly suitable for a category were included. Moreover, while hundreds of them are innocuous, a large number are considered by both adults and children to be taboo or profane. Even so, many children have been able to remain technically free from profanity in reciting such daring lines as "*Go to Hel*ena, Arkansas, where your hat *got dam*aged."

Teacher-Child Rhymes

1. Ashes to ashes
    Dust to dust,
    If Latin doesn't get us,
    Algebra must.

2. From the shores of Mr. _____'s desk
    To the halls of bubble gum bay,
    We'll fight our country's battles
    With spitballs, mud and clay.
    First you fight for lunch and recess
    And to keep our desks a mess.
    We are proud to claim the title
    Of teacher's little pests.

    > *Usually sung to the tune of "Semper Fidelis."*

3. Glory, glory, Hallelujah,
    Teacher hit me with a ruler,
    Met her at the door with a loaded forty-four
    And there ain't no teacher any more.

    > *Usually sung to the tune of "Battle Hymn of the Republic."*

4. Mulberry leaves and calico sheaves,
    All good teachers are hard to please.

5. No more pencils, no more books,
   No more teachers' dirty looks.

6. Now I lay me down to rest,
   I pray I pass tomorrow's test;
   But if I die before I wake,
   That's one less test I have to take.

7. On top of Old Smoky,
   All covered with gum,
   I shot my dear teacher
   With a rubber-band gun;
   I shot her with glory,
   I shot her with pride.
   How could I miss her?
   She was sixty feet wide.
           Sung to the tune of "On Top of Old Smoky."

8. Remember the fight,
   Remember the fun;
   Remember the homework
   That never got done.

9. School's out, school's out,
   Teacher's let the mules[1] out.

---

1. Variant: monkeys.

10. Teacher, teacher, don't whip me,
     Whip that boy behind that tree.
     He stole money, I stole honey,
     Teacher, teacher, ain't that funny!

11. Teacher, teacher, two by four,
     Can't get through the bathroom door.

12. Teacher, teacher, you're no preacher.
     Why do you scream and act so mean?

13. The bell rung, the bell rung,
     The teacher got her tail hung.

Child-Child Taunts

1. Baby, baby, suck your thumb,
    Wash your face in bubble gum.
    Hang 'em high, hang 'em low.
    Hang 'em in the picture show.

2. Cry, baby, cry,
    Stick your finger in your eye,
    Run and tell your mother
    That it was not I!

3. Cry your hat full,
   Cry toot!

4. Hello, hello, my darling child,
   Rich man ran away with the poor man's wife.
   The poor man ran in the corner and cried.

5. I know something I ain't gonna tell,
   Three little niggers in a coconut shell;
   One could read, and one could write,
   And one could smoke his daddy's pipe.

6. Rough, tough, cream puff!

7. Scaredy cat, scaredy cat,
   Stump your toe and eat a rat!

8. Tattletale, tattletale,
   Hanging on a bull's tail,
   Ninety-nine hundred feet long.

9. Tattletale, tattletale,
   Hang your britches on a nail,
   Hang 'em high, hang 'em low,
   Hang 'em in the picture show.

Taunts During Hiding Games

1. *A B C*
   A B C, tumbled down *D*.
   Cat's in the cupboard
   And you can't catch me

2. Can't catch me,
   Can't catch a flea
   On a bumble bee.

3. Kitty cat, kitty cat,
   Can't catch me.

4. You can't catch me,
   Because you're only ninety-three.

5. You can't find the red side of a blue barn.

6. You missed me, you missed me,
   Now you've got to kiss me.

Retorts to Playmates

1. *To a silly question.*
   Ask a silly question and I give you a silly answer.

2. *What's your name?*
   Buster Brown,
   Ask me again and I'll knock you down.

3. *What's your name?*
   Pudd'n and Tame,
   . Ask me again and I'll tell you the same.

4. *When a child asks "What for?" (pronounced "fur")*
   Cat fur, kitten britches. You want a pair?

5. *To one who asks personal questions.*
   Curiosity killed the cat. Don't you feel sick?

6. *If a child is shy and won't talk.*
   Has the cat got your tongue?

7. *To egg a playmate on.*
   I dare you, I dare you, I double dog dare you!

8. *To a pouting playmate.*
   Pick up your lip before I step on it.

9. *To make a child feel rejected.*
   Smarty, smarty, had a party,
   Nobody came but smarty, smarty.

10. *To a personal question.*
That's for me to know and you to find out.

11. *A challenge to race.*
The last one in is a rotten egg![2]

12. *To a vain child.*
Yes, you're pretty. Pretty ugly and pretty apt to stay that way.

13. *When a child brags.*
You'll do wonders and plunders and eat rotten cucumbers.

14. *To incite a child.*
Your mama is on the chain gang.[3]

15. *When a boy's fly is open.*
You're going to let your horse out.[4]

16. *To the last one in a race.*
You're the cow tail.

---

2. Variant: green pig.

3. Variants: Your sister (or mother) wears army boots. Your mother drives a pickle wagon.

4. Variant: Your trap door is open.

Miscellany

1. Blue, blue, you have the flu;
   I don't want to play with you.

2. Buster Brown went to town
   With his britches upside down.

3. Fatty, Fatty, two by four,
   Couldn't get through a ten-foot door.

4. Georgy, Porgy, pudd'n and pie,
   Kissed the girls and made them cry;
   He swung on a rope and got away,
   We'll get Georgy another day.

5. Goody, goody, gout,
   Your shirt tail's out,
   Goody, goody, gin,
   Put it in again.

6. Happy birthday to you;
   You belong in the zoo.
   You look like a monkey,
   And you smell like one too.

7. Here comes the bride,
    Look how she wobbles from side to side;
    The groom's skinny as a broom,
    Walks like he has no room.

8. Hi ho, hi ho,
    It's off to school we go,
    With razor blades and hand grenades,
    Hi, hi, hi, ho!

9. I eat my peas with honey,
    I've done it all my life;
    It makes my peas taste funny,
    But it keeps them on the knife.

10. I saw you in the ocean,
    I saw you in the sea,
    I saw you in the bathtub,
    Oops! Pardon me!

11. I see Christmas, I see toys,
    I see _____'s dirty drawers.

12. I see London, I see France,
    I see _____'s dirty pants.

13. I'm a cool, cool mommy
    From a cool, cool town;
    It takes a cool, cool man
    To cool mommy down.

14. I'm Popeye the sailor man, poo, poo!
    I live in the garbage can, poo, poo!
    I even go swimming with bowlegged women,
    I'm Popeye the sailor man, poo, poo!

15. Jingle bells, shotgun shells,
    Granny had a gun;
    Shot me through the underwear
    And, boy, I had to run!

16. Johnny, Johnny, strong and able,
    Get your elbow off the table.

17. Look up, look down, look around,
    I see your pants hanging down.

18. Mary had a little car,
    It was bright, bright red,
    But everywhere that Mary went,
    The cops picked up the dead!

19. Mary had a little lamb,
    But now the lamb is dead,
    She carries it to school each day,
    Between two chunks of bread.

20. Mrs. Brown looks like a clown,
    I wish her pants would fall down.

21. Now I lay me down to sleep,
    With my hot rod in the street.
    If it should roll before I wake,
    I pray the Lord to pull the brake.

22. Oh, little hippie,
    Come out and smoke with me,
    Bring your LSD,
    Climb up my marijuana tree,
    Slide down my razor,
    Into my beer can
    And we'll be jolly friends
    Forever more, more, more.

23. Peas and cornbread had a fight,
    Peas knocked the cornbread out of sight.
    Cornbread said, "That's all right,
    I'll get you tomorrow night."

24. Red, green, and yellow,
     He's a bad fellow.

25. Red, white, and blue,
     The monkey favors you.

26. Red, yellow, and white,
     You're a terrible sight.

27. Tiddledy, daddledy, baddledy boo,
     I am me but who are you?

28. Yankee Doodle went to town
     Riding on a turtle,
     Turned the corner just in time
     To see a lady's girdle.

29. Yes ma'am, no ma'am
     Thankee ma'am, please,
     Slice the turkey
     And pass the peas.